# Big Dots.
# Little Dots.
## The Elements of Art.

Written & Illustrated by

Vivian Magarino-Gomez

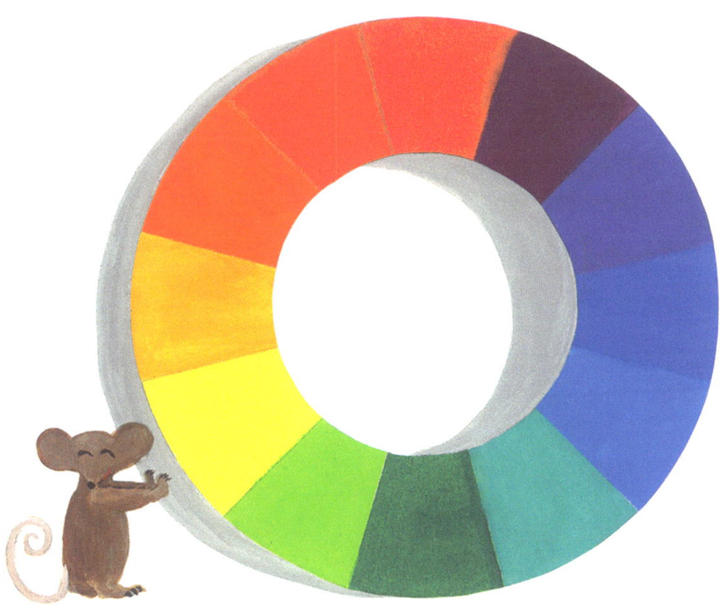

Little Earthling Press™

*For Olivia, Norberto, Amanda and Sophia*



Little Earthling Press™

http://www.WelcomeEarthling.com

Printed in the United States

Library of Congress Control Number: 2013904925

Summary: Teaching art concept to children: early child development and elementary education, elements of art with interdisciplinary links to science and math concepts.

Library of Congress subject heading:
Elements of art, Arts-Study and teaching, Elementary art education, Arts in Math and Science education.

ISBN-978-0-9886030-0-4 (EB)

ISBN-978-0-9886030-1-1 (PB)

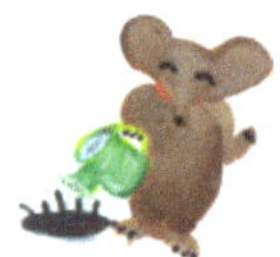

Dear Parents and Caregivers,

This book can be read to even the youngest of children. Basic constructs are defined and can be revisited for deeper understanding as your child grows.

The glossary in the back of the book reviews the relevant art, math, and science concepts. As you read, briefly introduce these concepts and examine the illustrations with your child to improve comprehension.

Asking questions about what they observe in an illustration can help children independently formulate correct answers and apply the information in real situations. This type of questioning accesses children's previous knowledge. For example, to help identify the warm colors, ask what colors your child would use to paint the sun? Or to identify vertical and horizontal lines, ask what kind of lines can your child sees in a door?

And lastly, extend learning by casually pointing out examples of these concepts in daily life. Art, science, and math are all around us. Enjoy the discovery!

Sincerest Thanks,

Vivian Magarino-Gomez

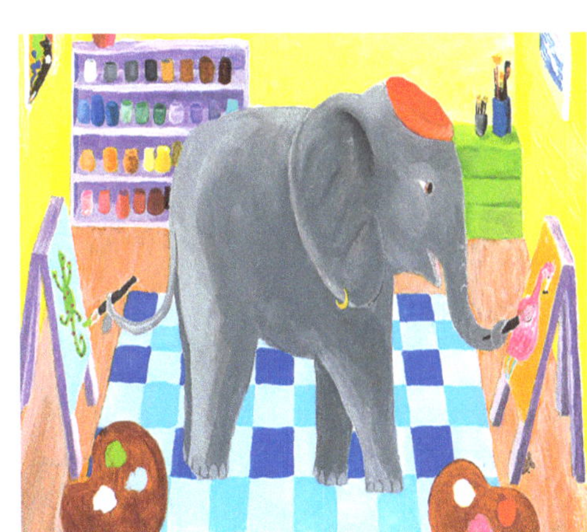

# The Elements of Art

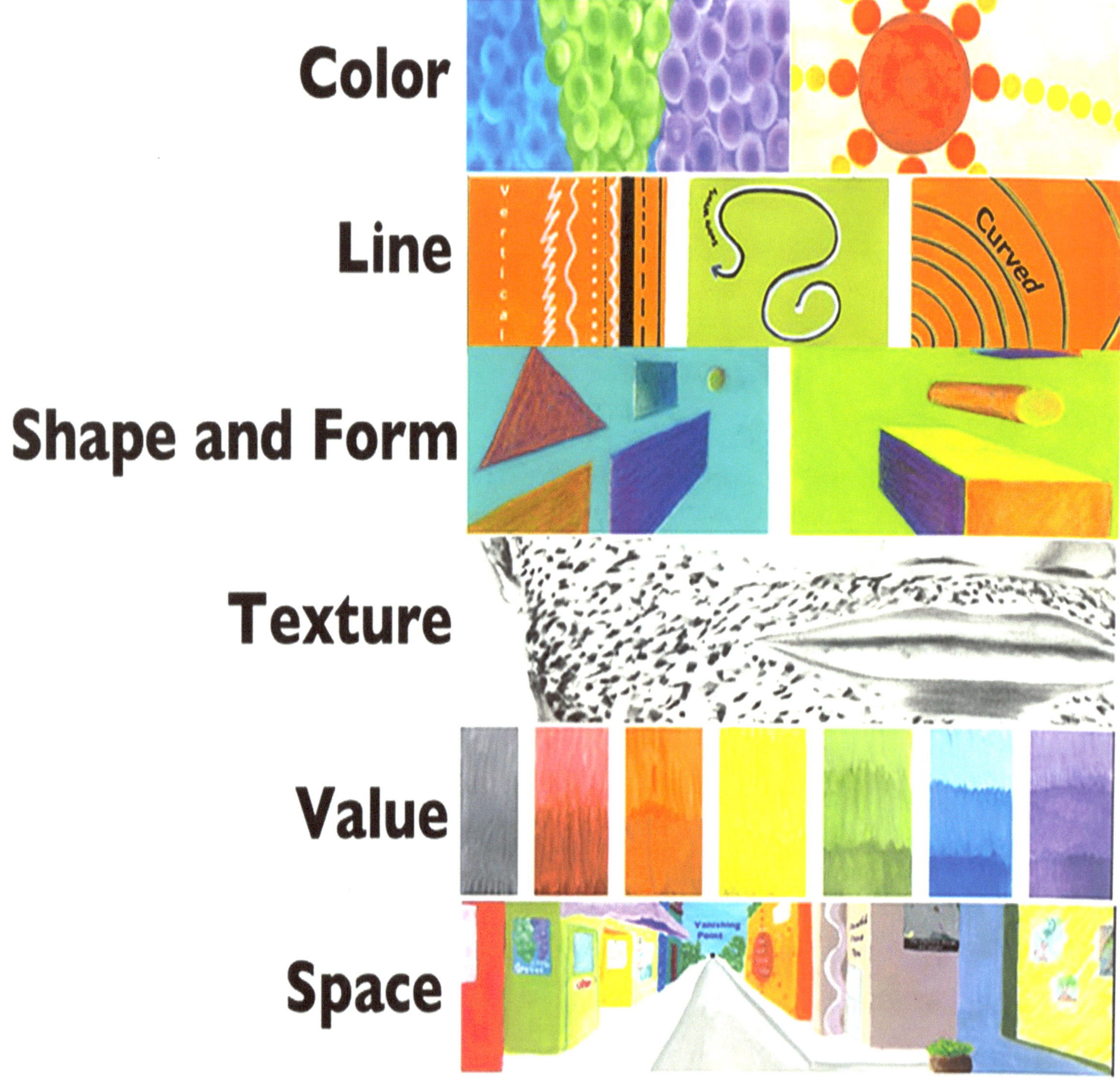

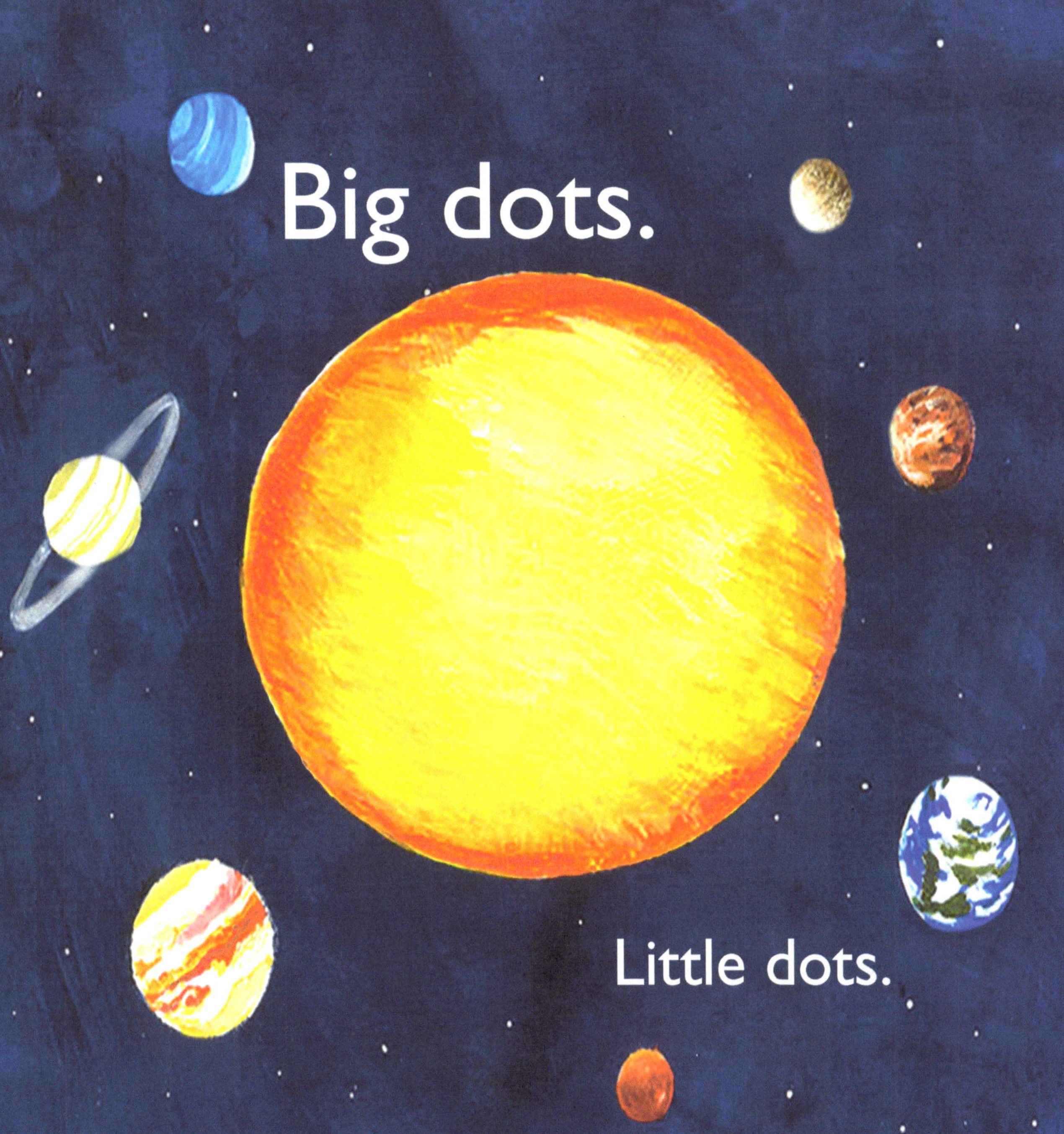
Big dots.
Little dots.

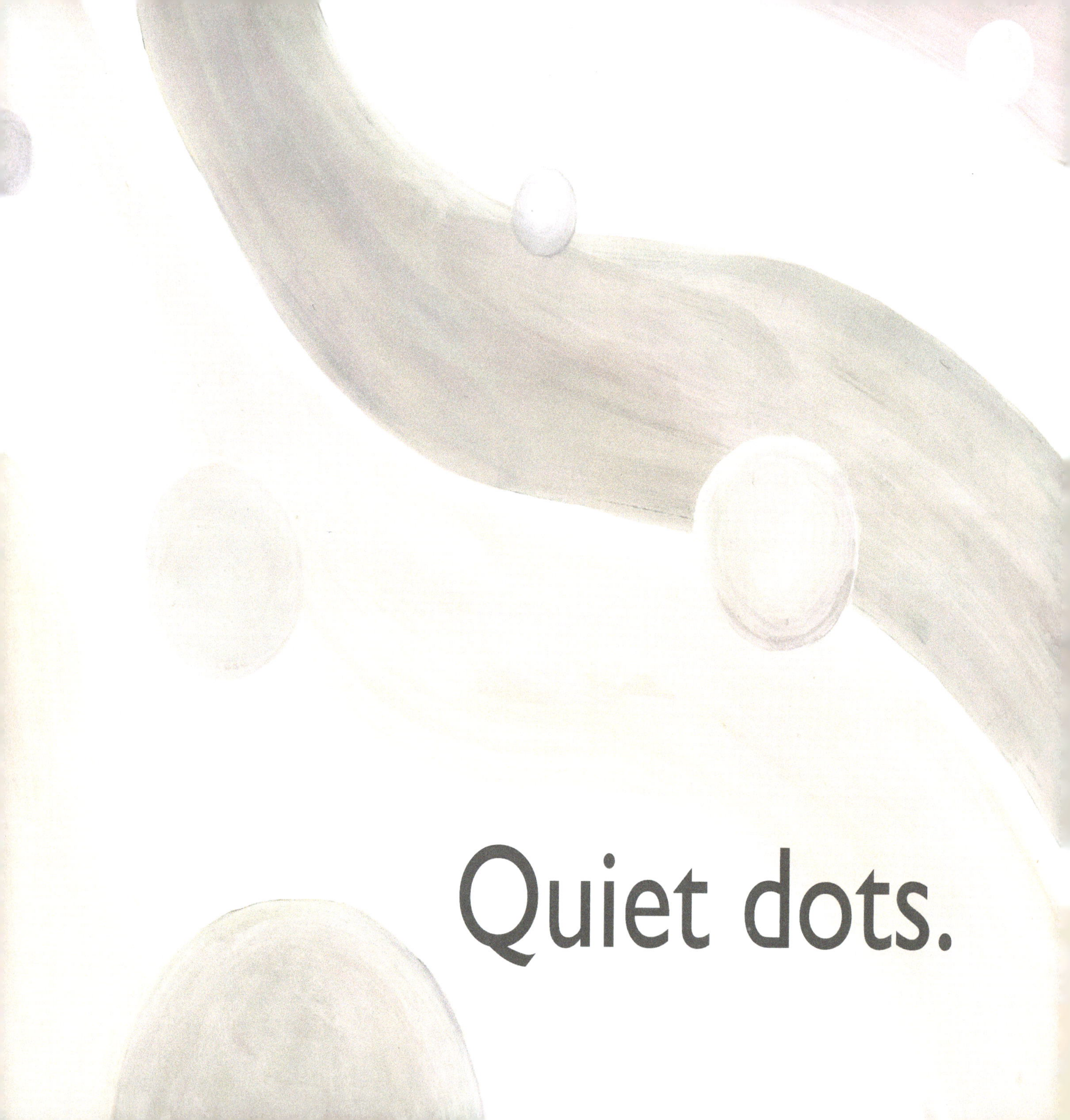

Quiet dots.

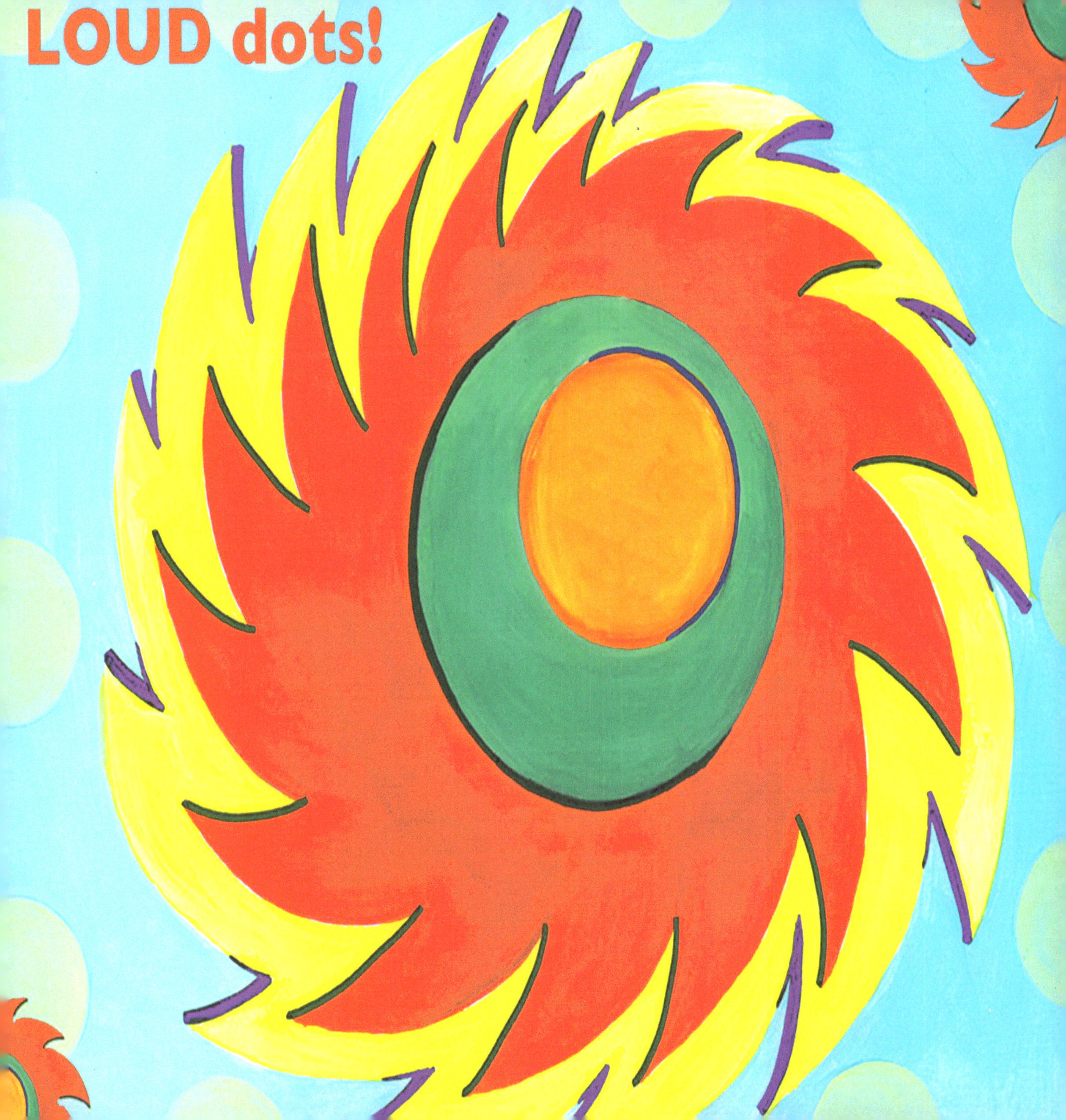
LOUD dots!

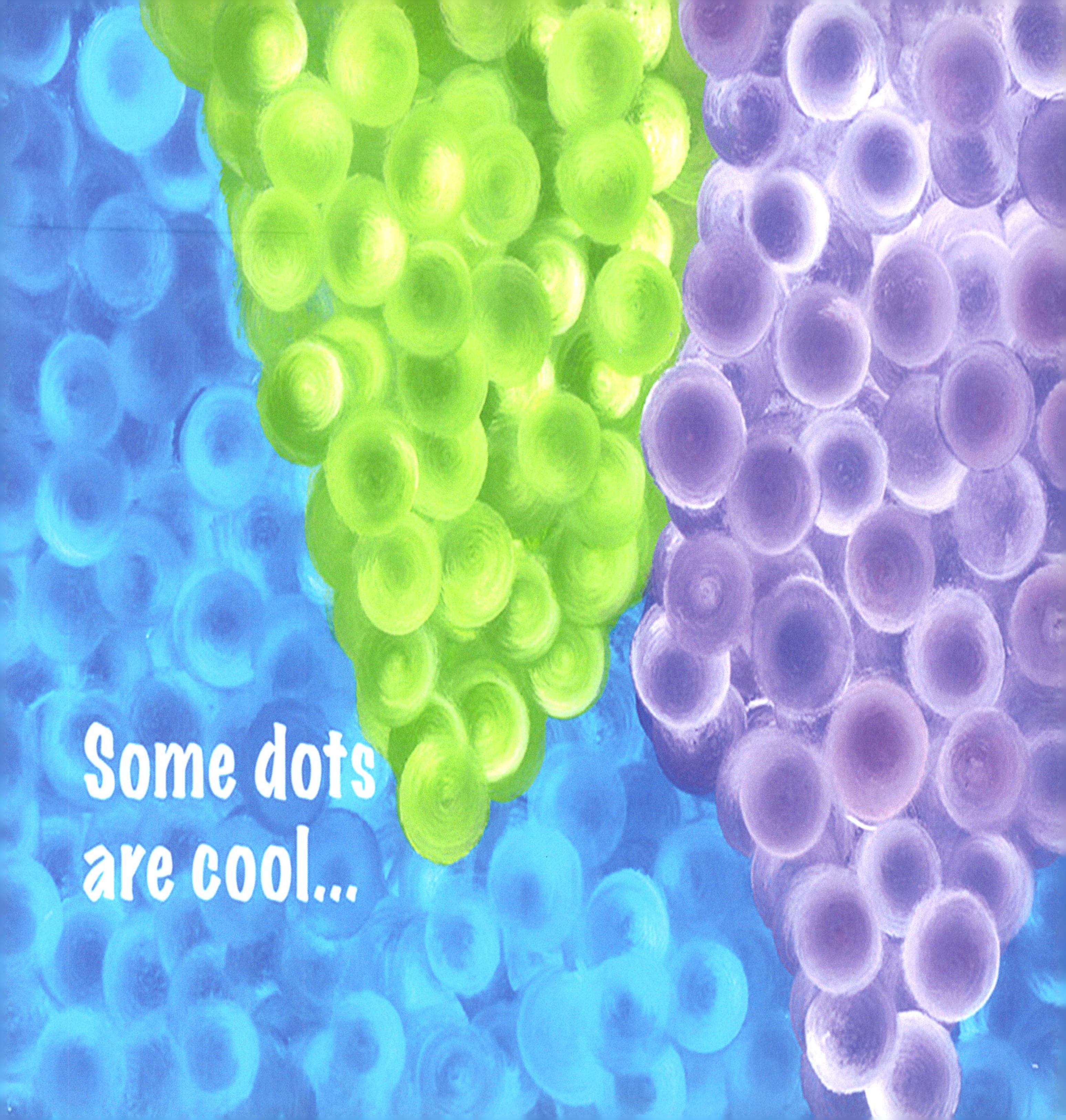
Some dots
are cool...

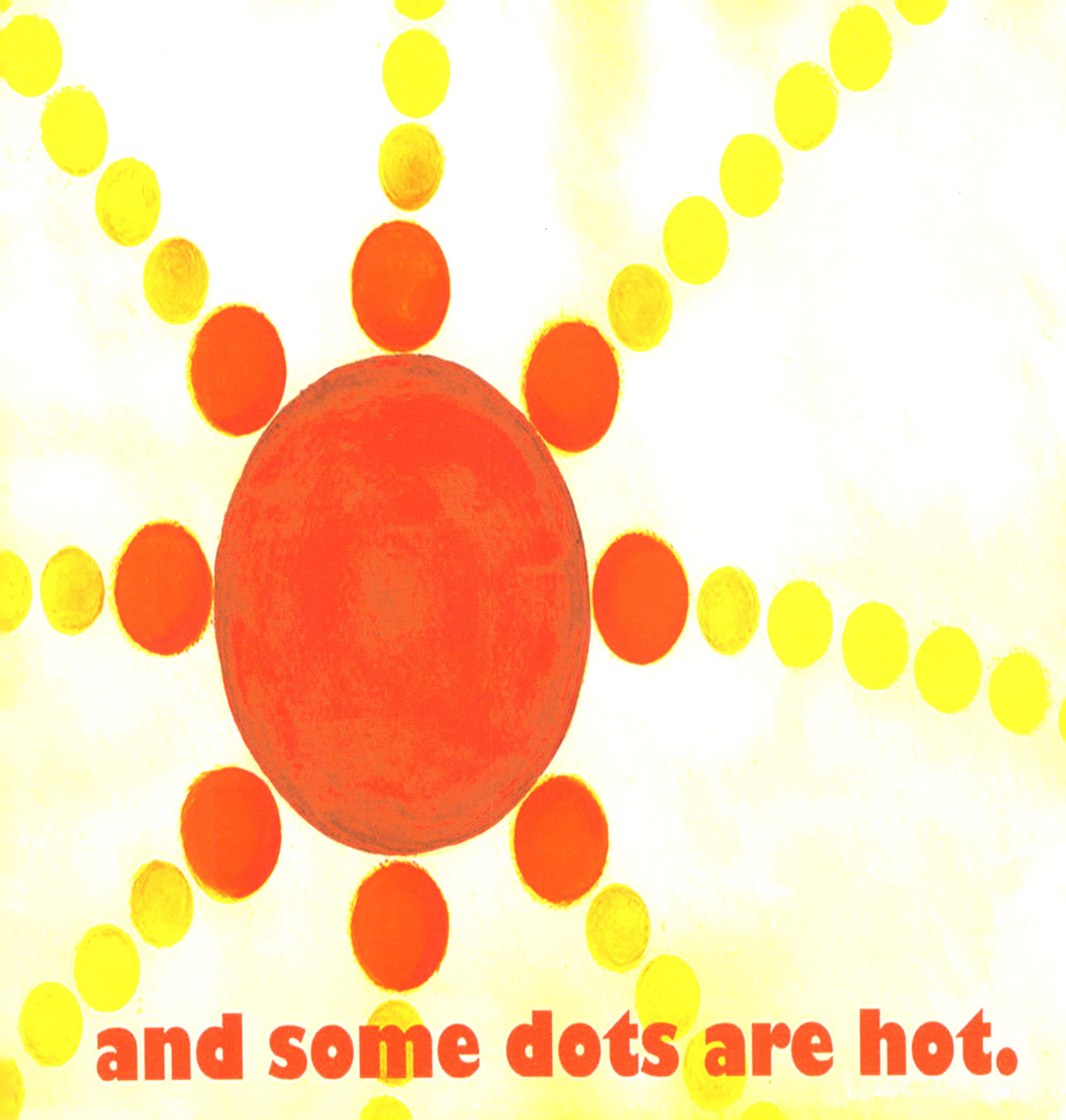
and some dots are hot.

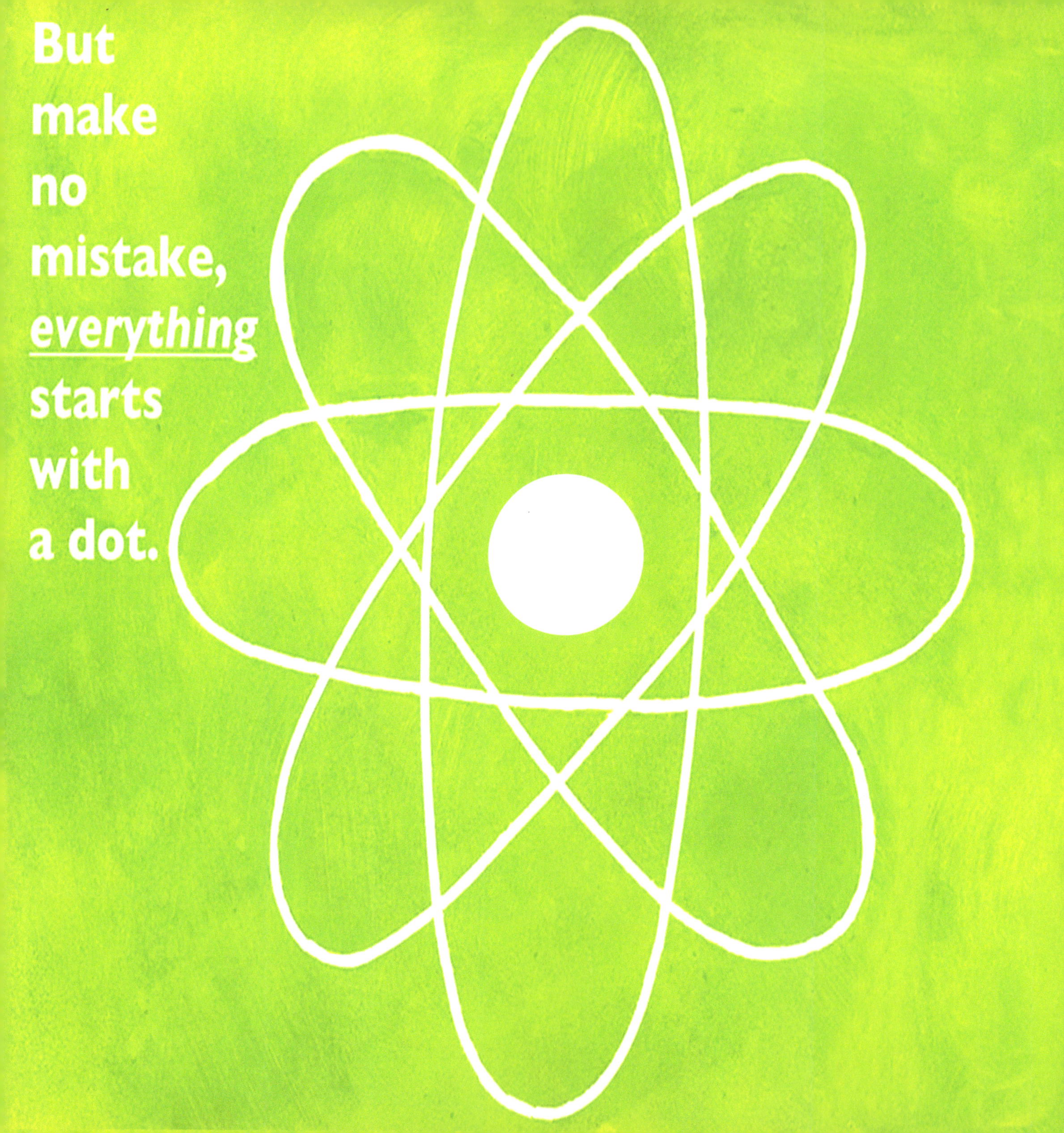
But
make
no
mistake,
everything
starts
with
a dot.

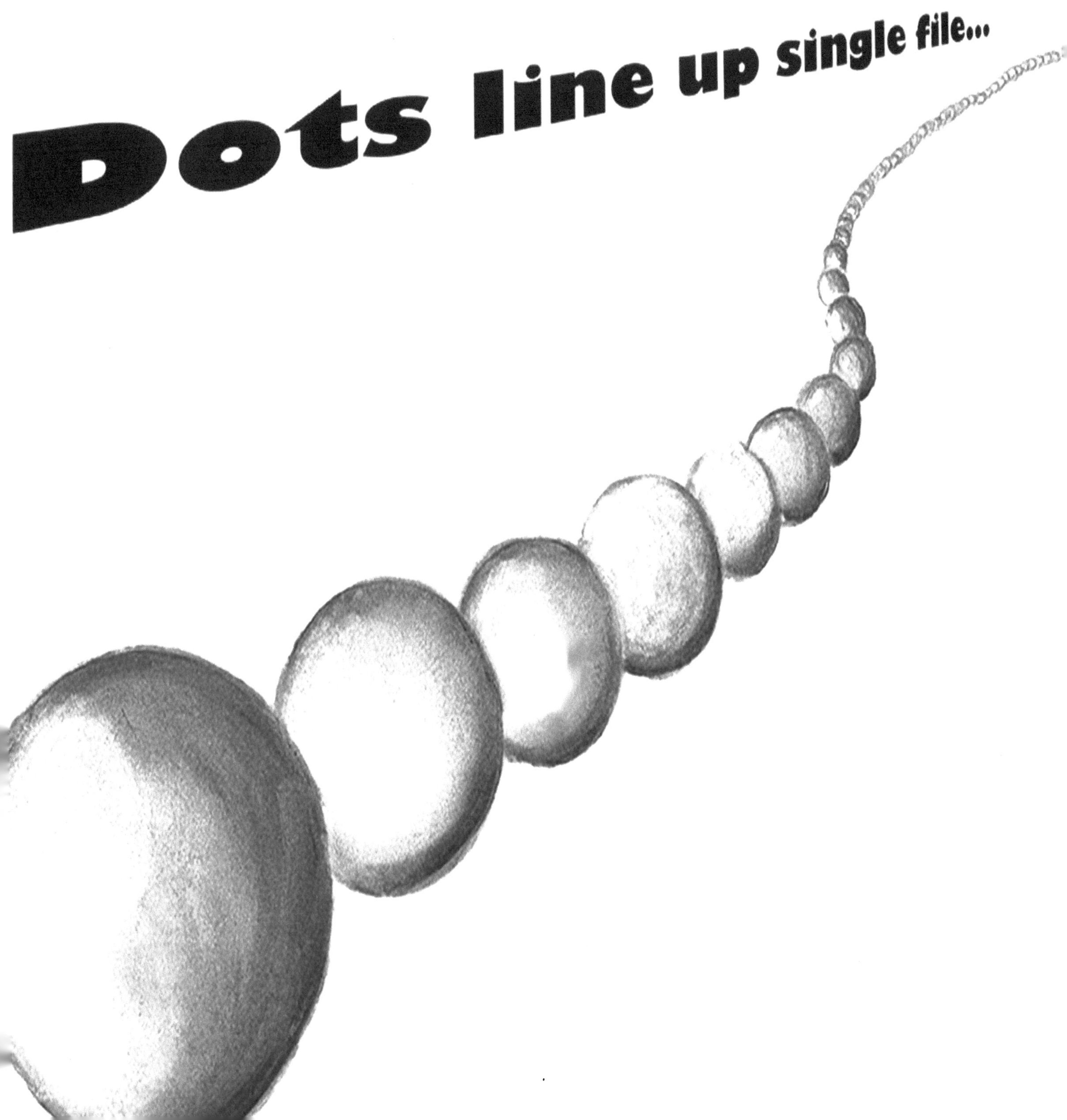
Dots line up single file...

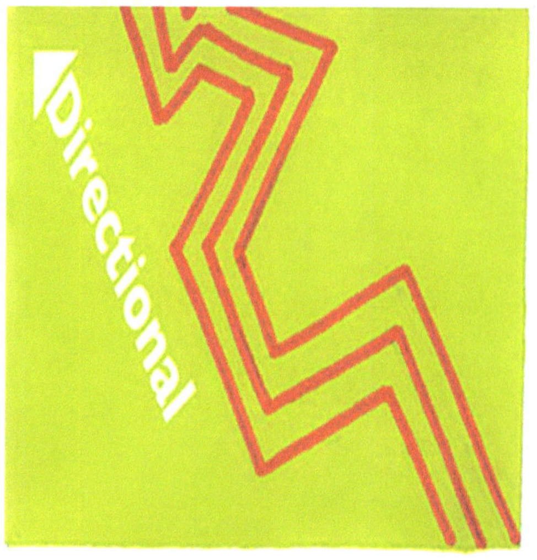


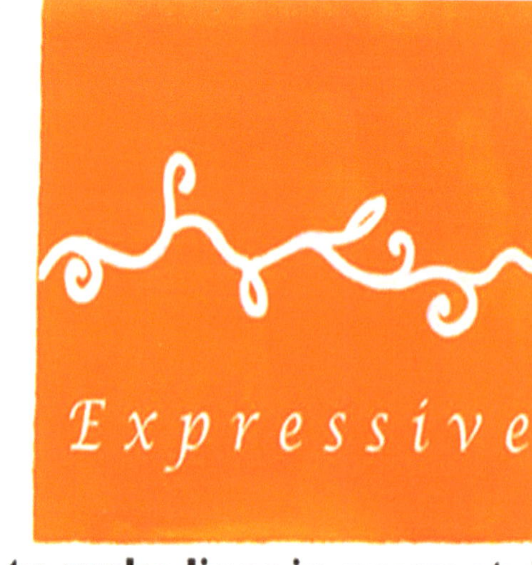


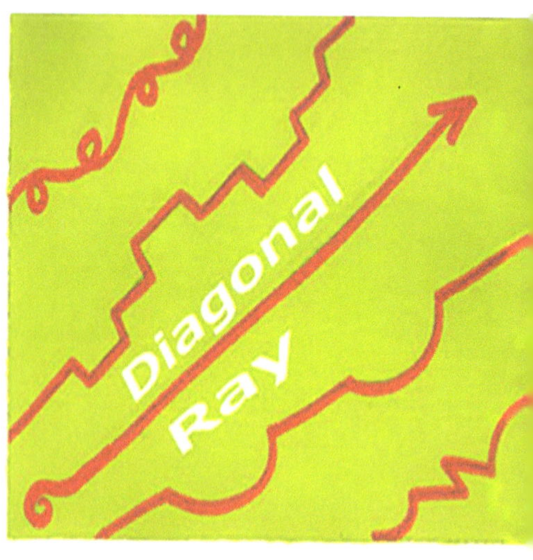


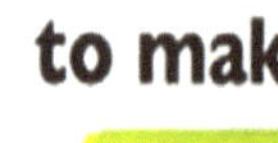

to make lines in every style.

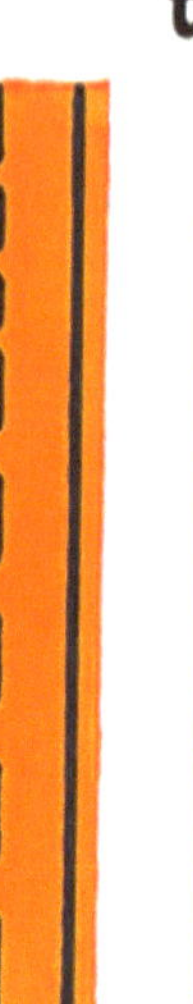


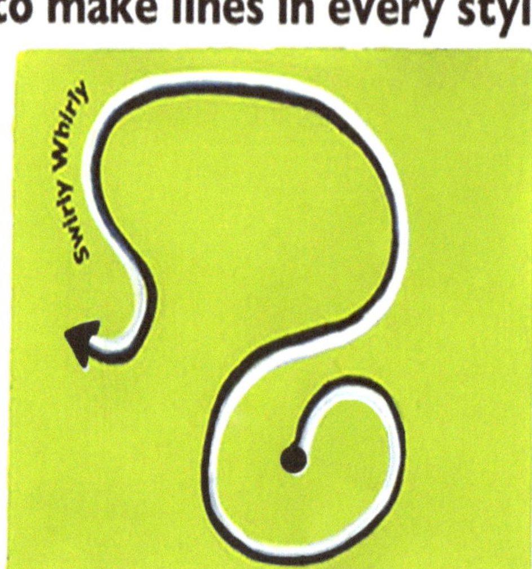


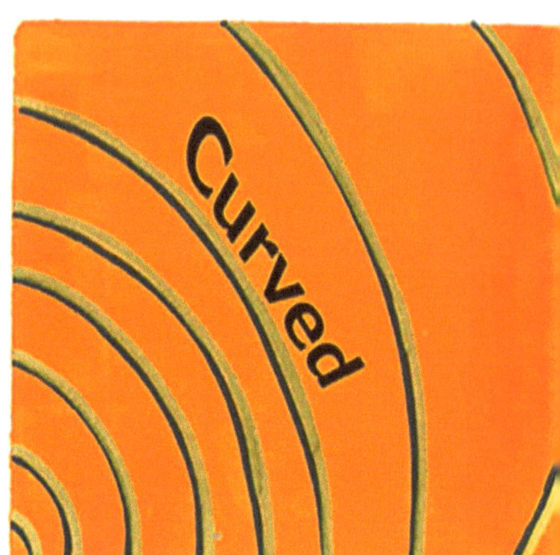


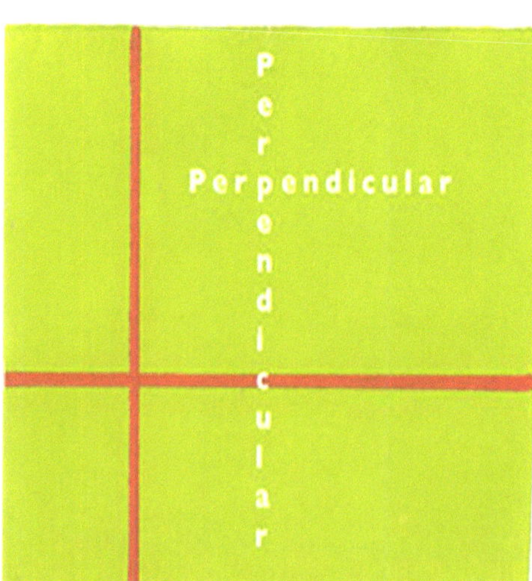


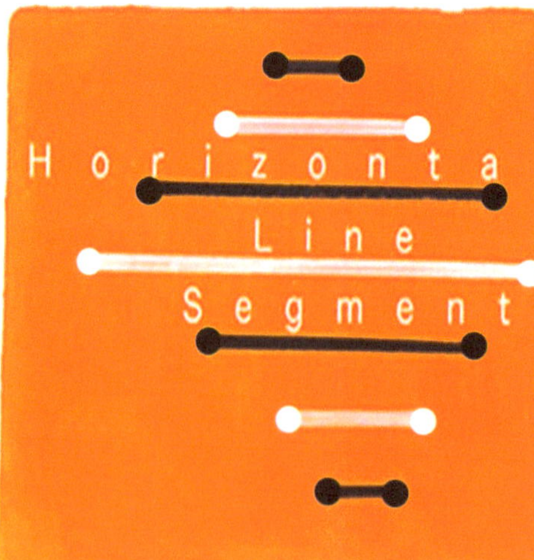

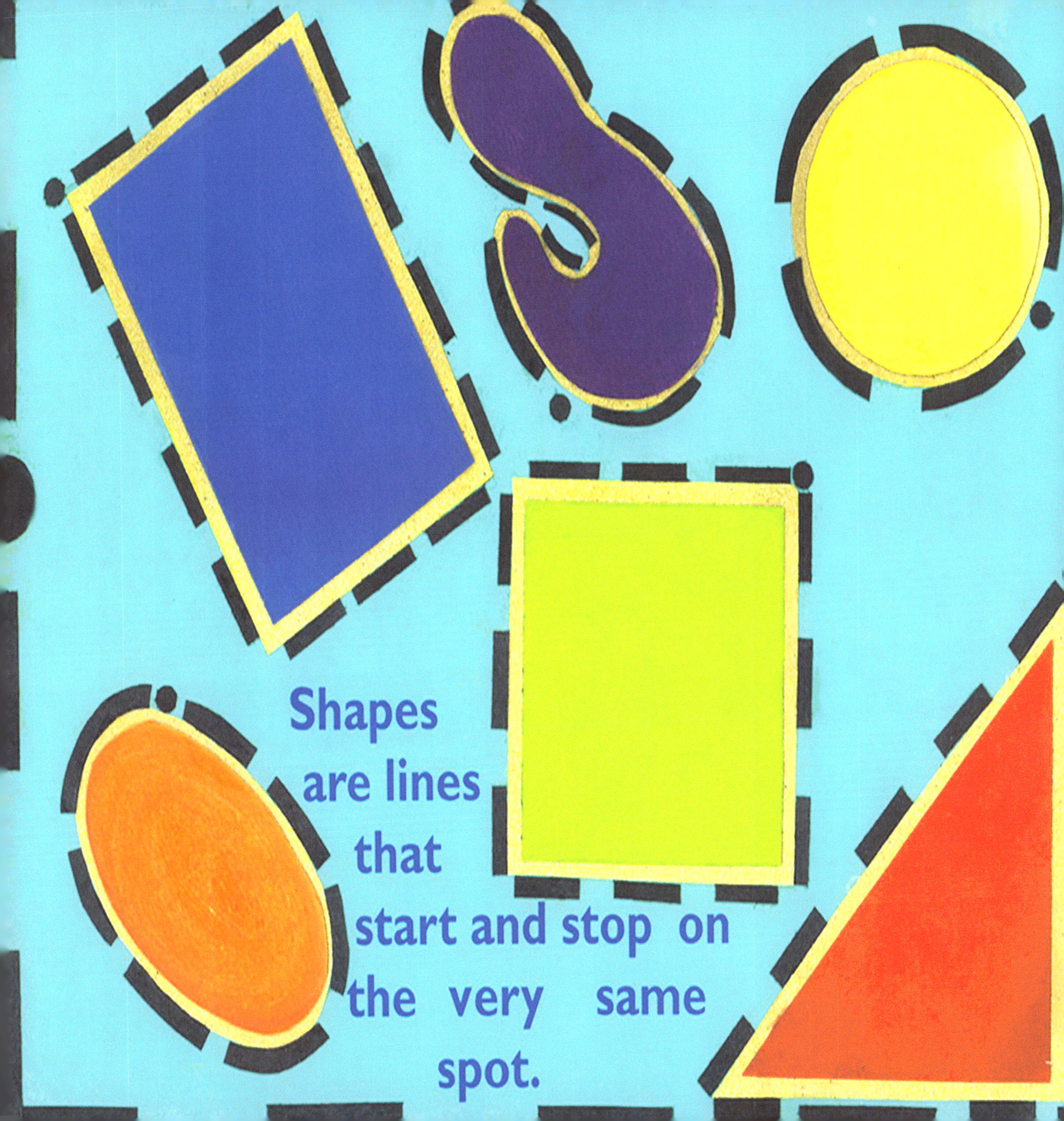
Shapes
are lines
that
start and stop on
the very same
spot.

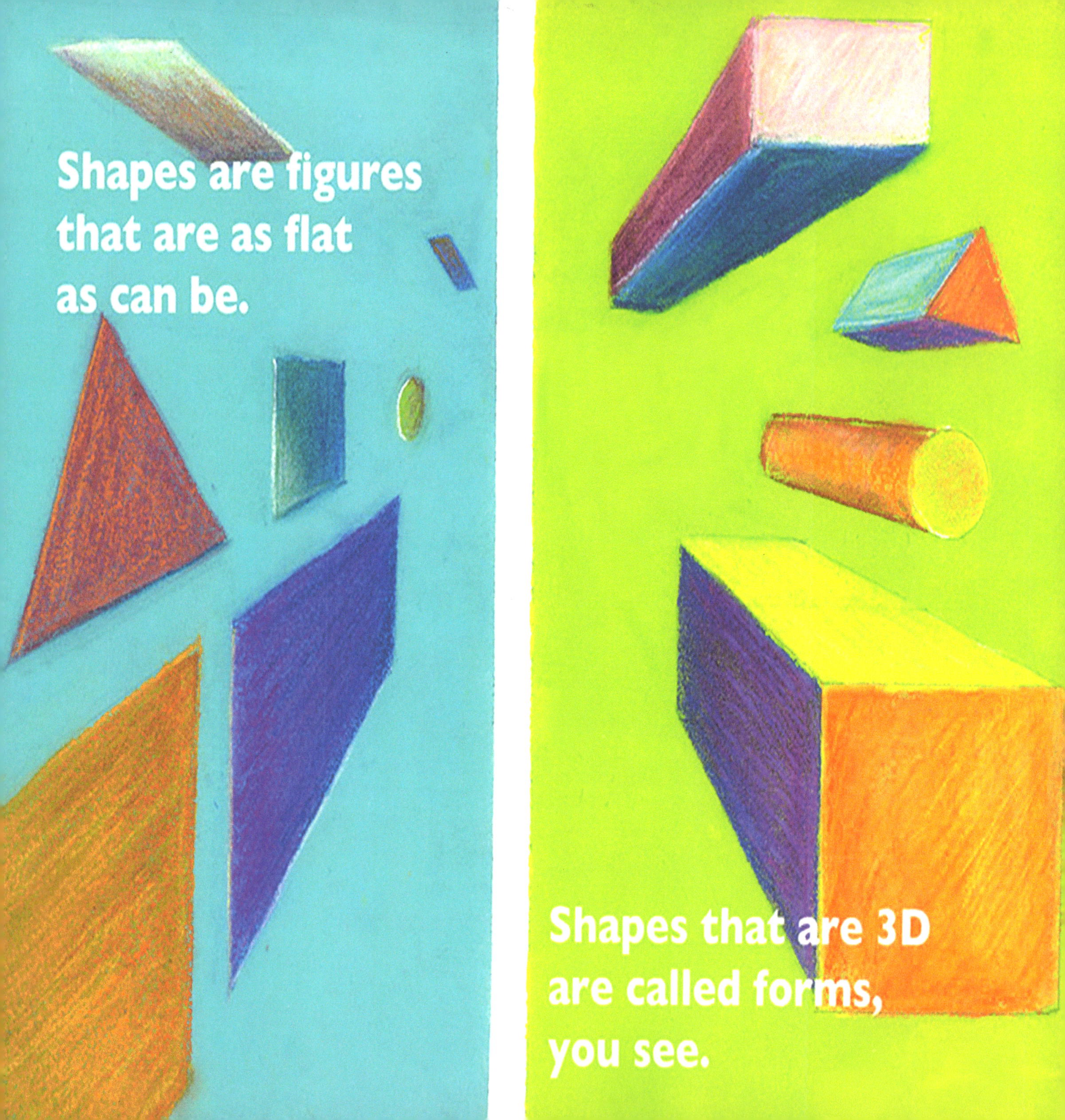
Shapes are figures that are as flat as can be.
Shapes that are 3D are called forms, you see.

Blow up
a circle
and
you
have a
ball.

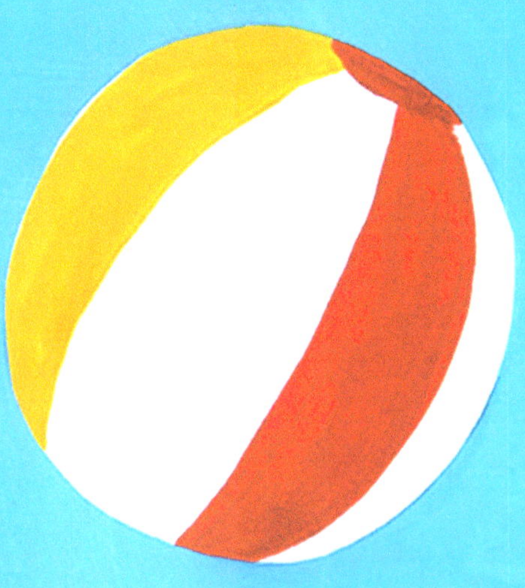

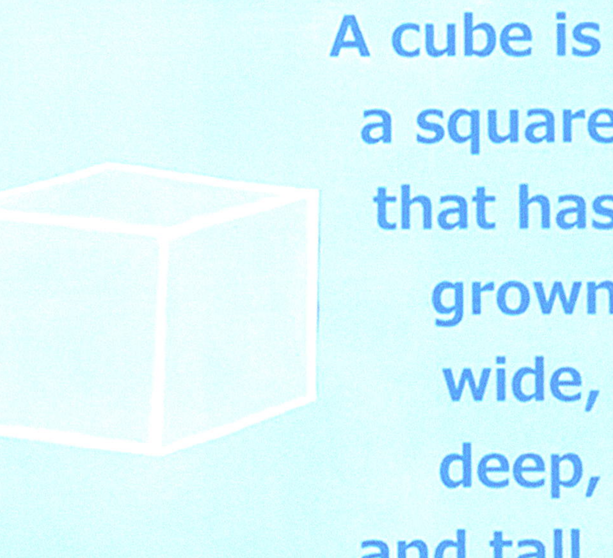

A cube is
a square
that has
grown
wide,
deep,
and tall.

Dots! Dots!
It's all about dots!

How to draw them
so they grow hair.

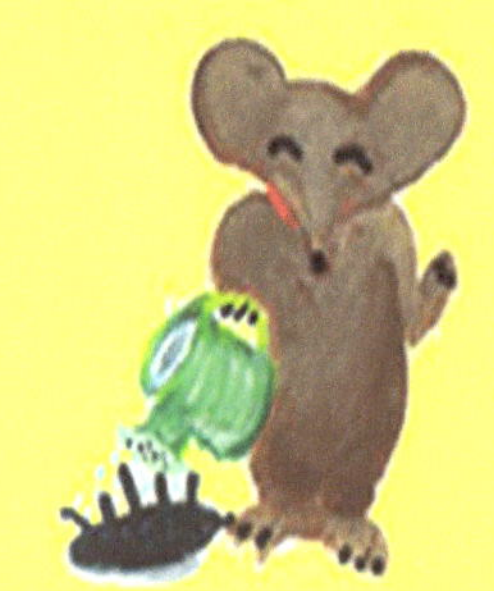

What's that you say there?

Draw
it right,
and it
looks like
daddy
needs
a shave.

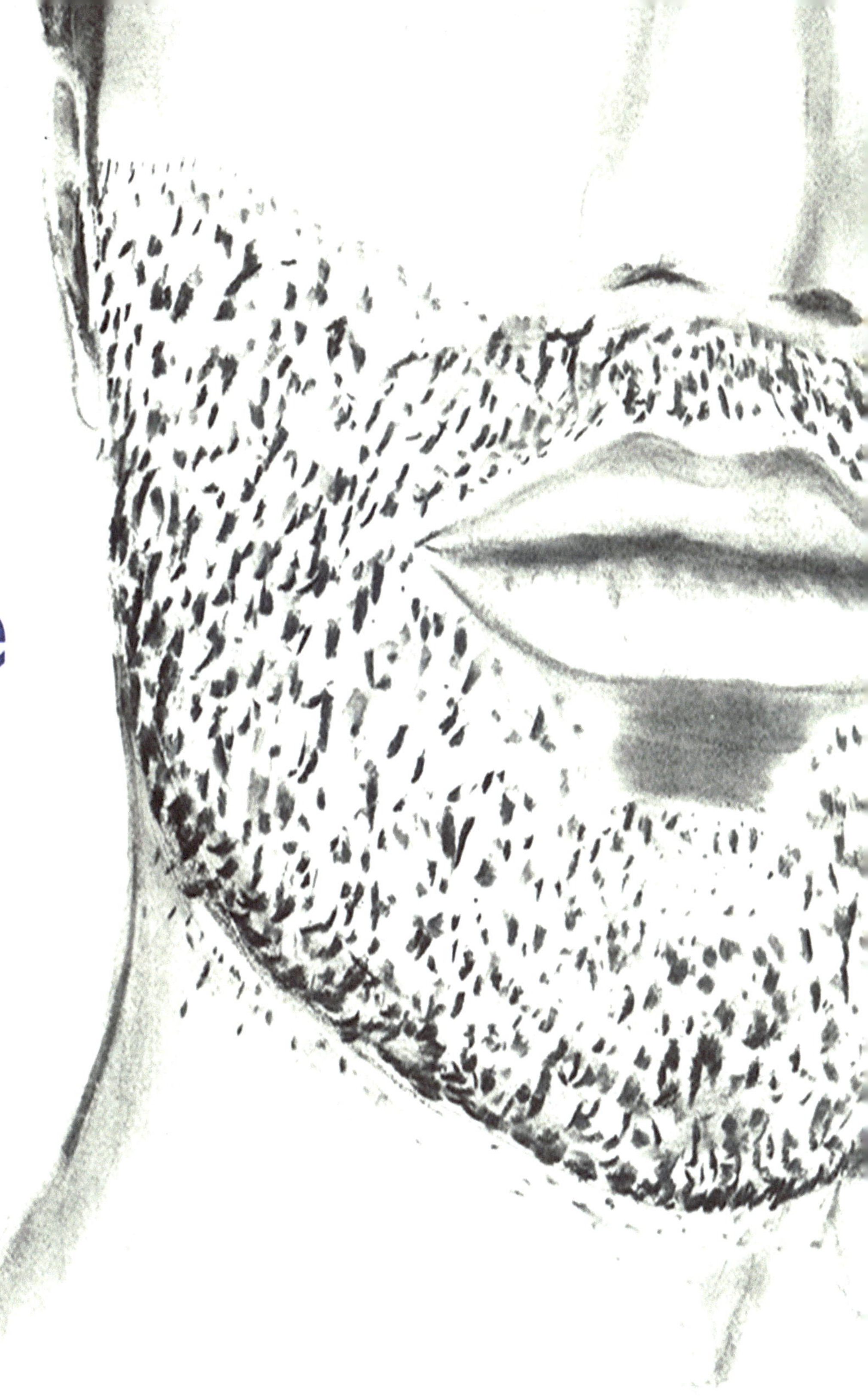

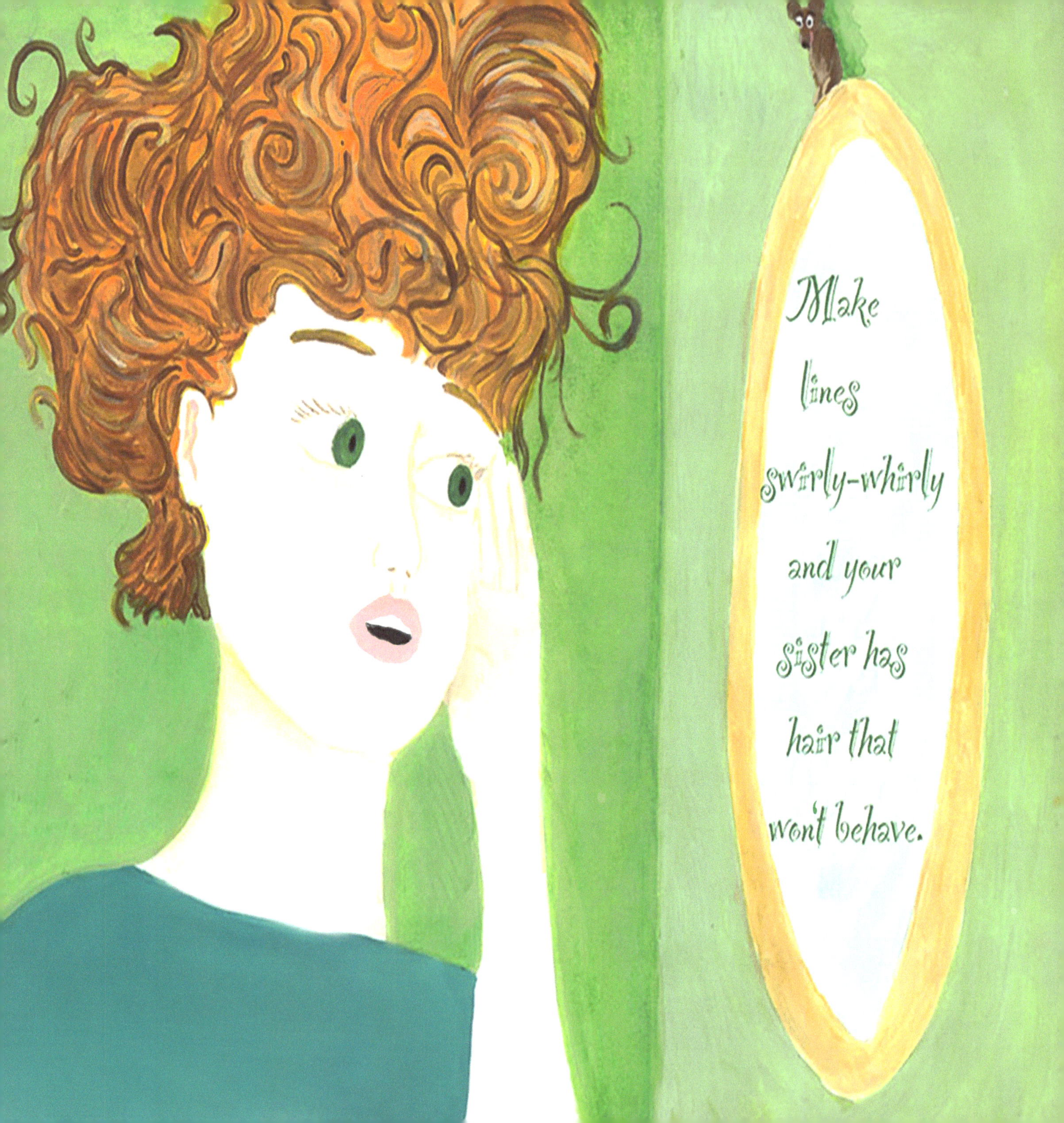
Make
lines
swirly-whirly
and your
sister has
hair that
won't behave.

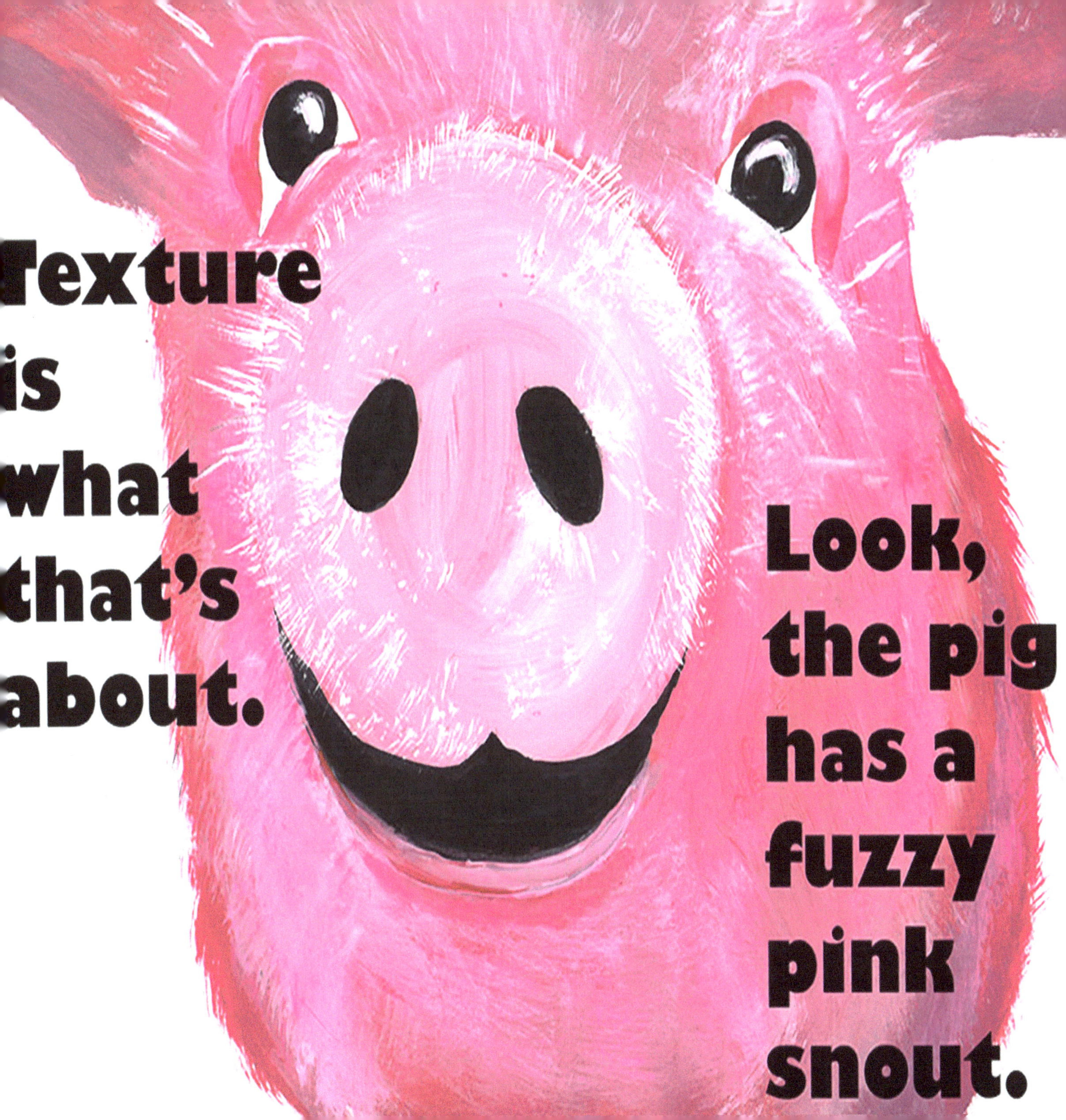

Texture
is
what
that's
about.

Look,
the pig
has a
fuzzy
pink
snout.

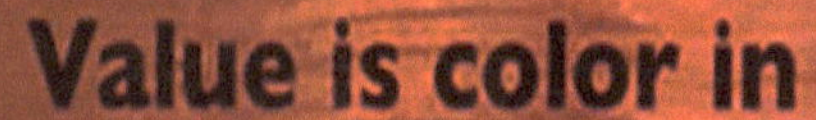

Value is color in

DARK, MEDIUM, and LIGHT.

It all depends if you
add black or white.

Shade or tint?

Here's a hint.

Just add black and white....

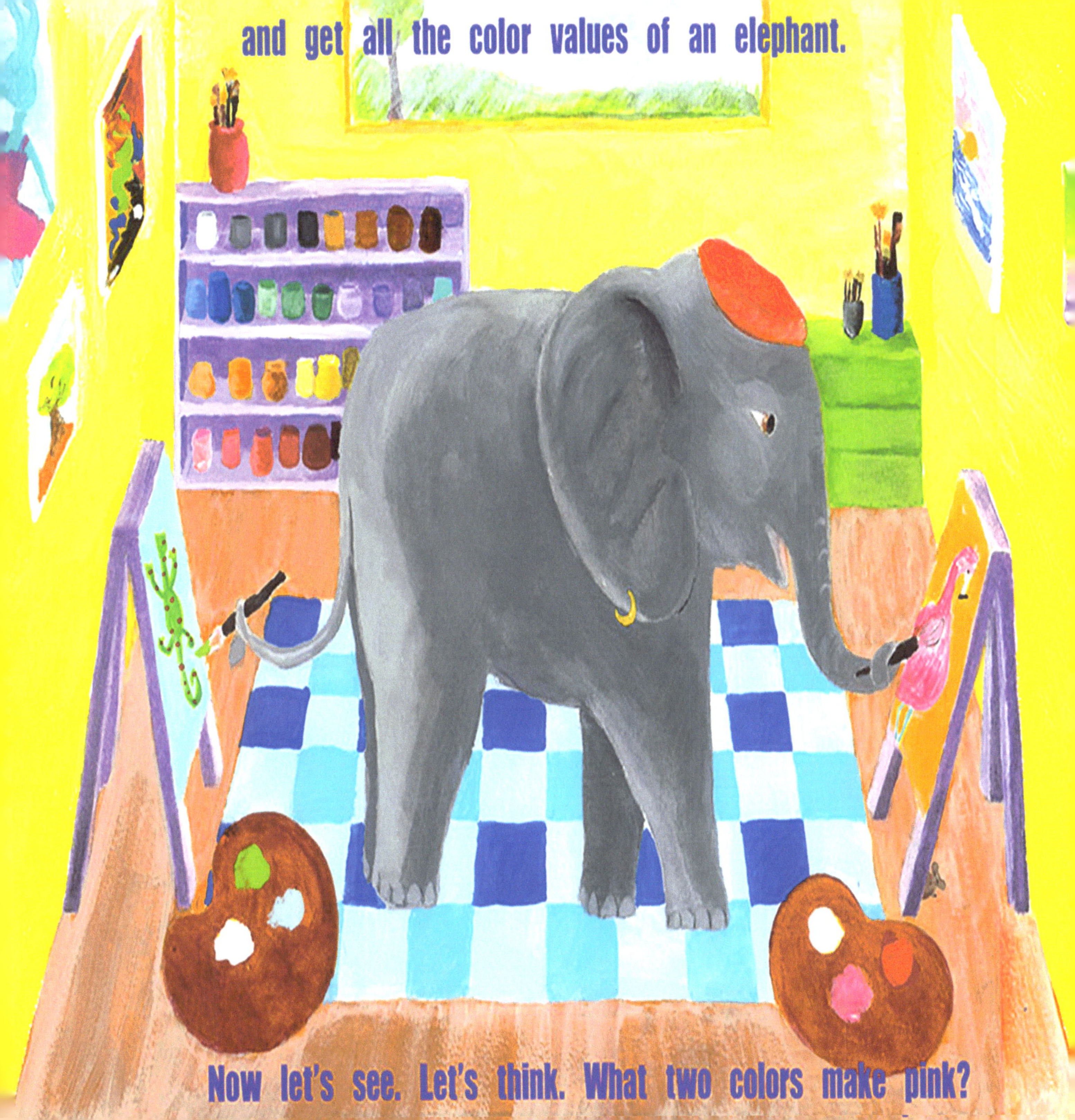

and get all the color values of an elephant.

Now let's see. Let's think. What two colors make pink?

Now think about spaces. Let's find dots some good places.

Where to put a dot
and where not

or way over there,

Close together,

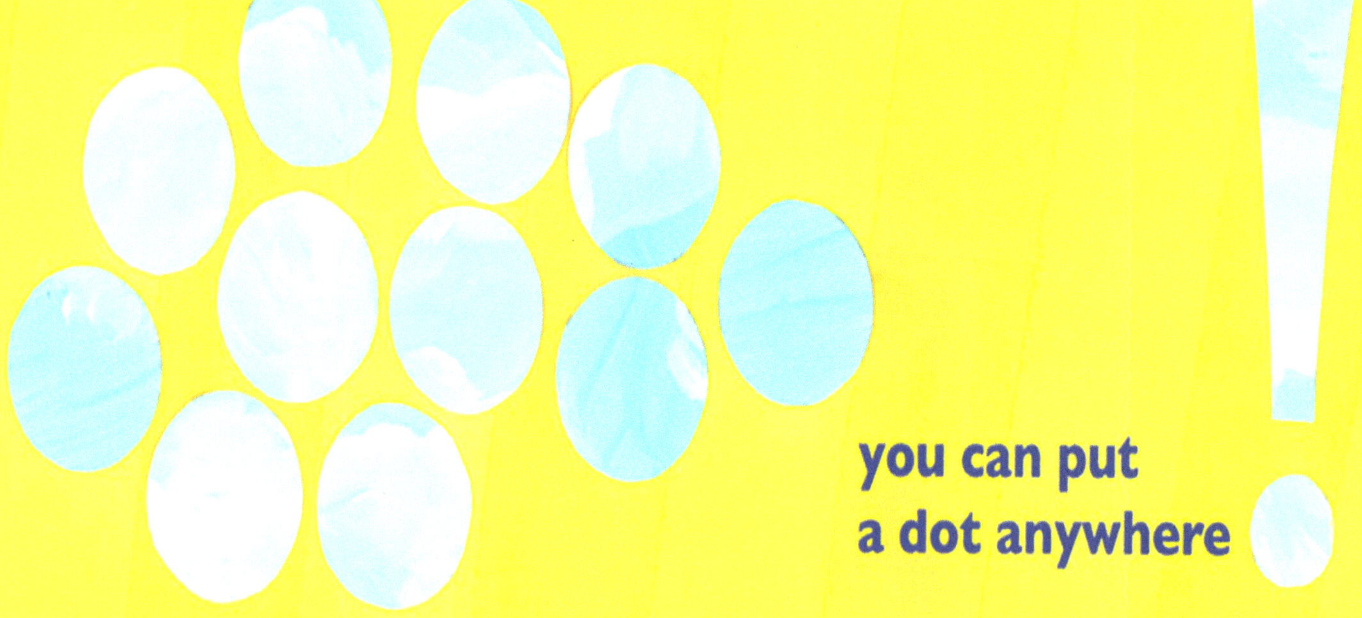

you can put
a dot anywhere

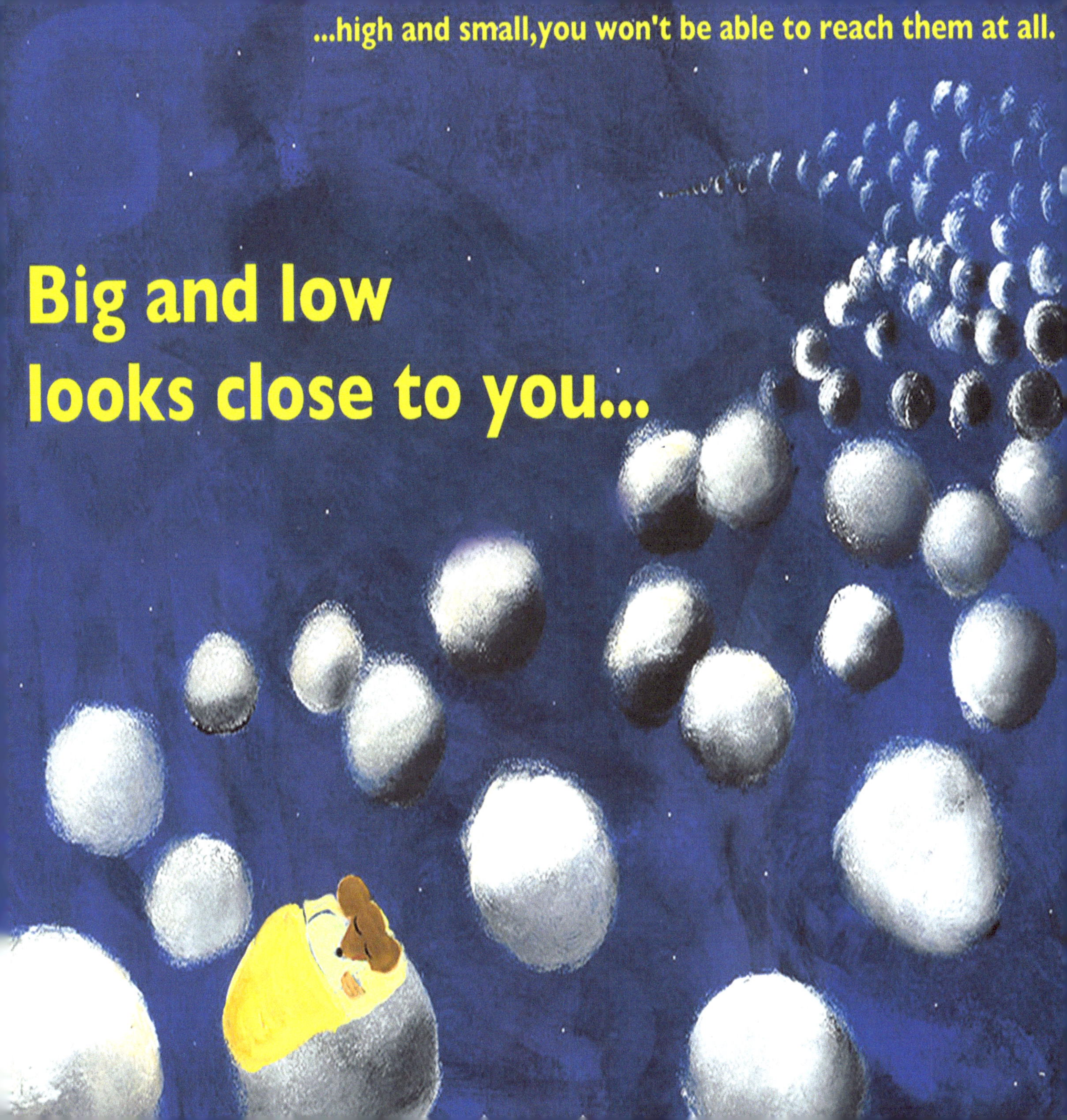
...high and small,you won't be able to reach them at all.
Big and low
looks close to you...

# Now where can we put these dots on our page?

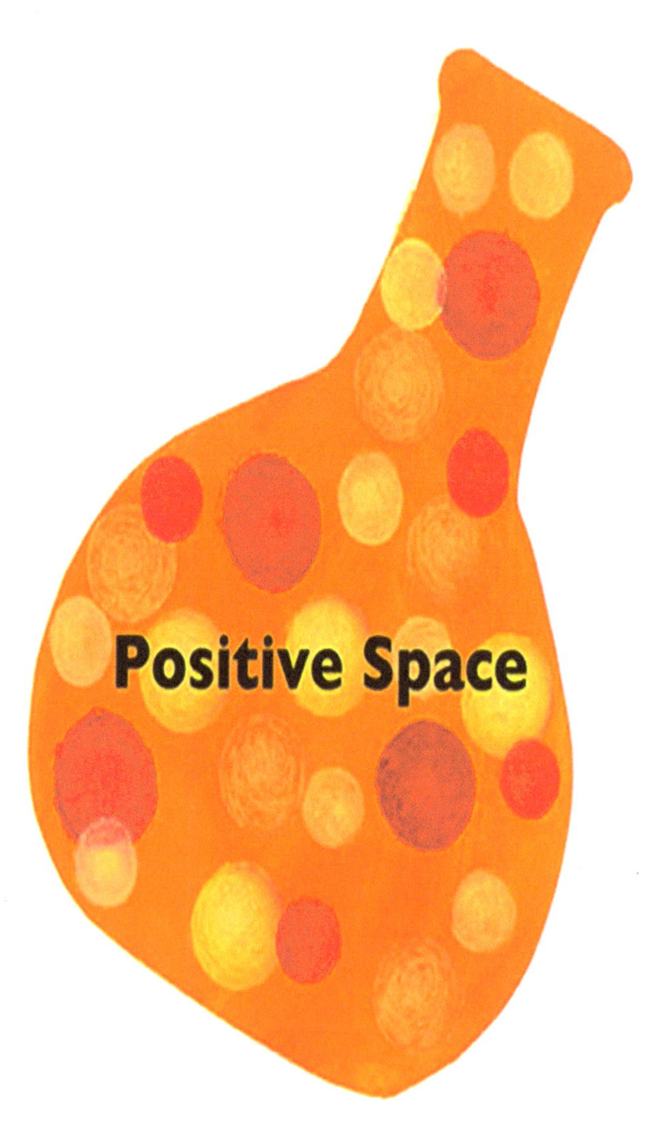

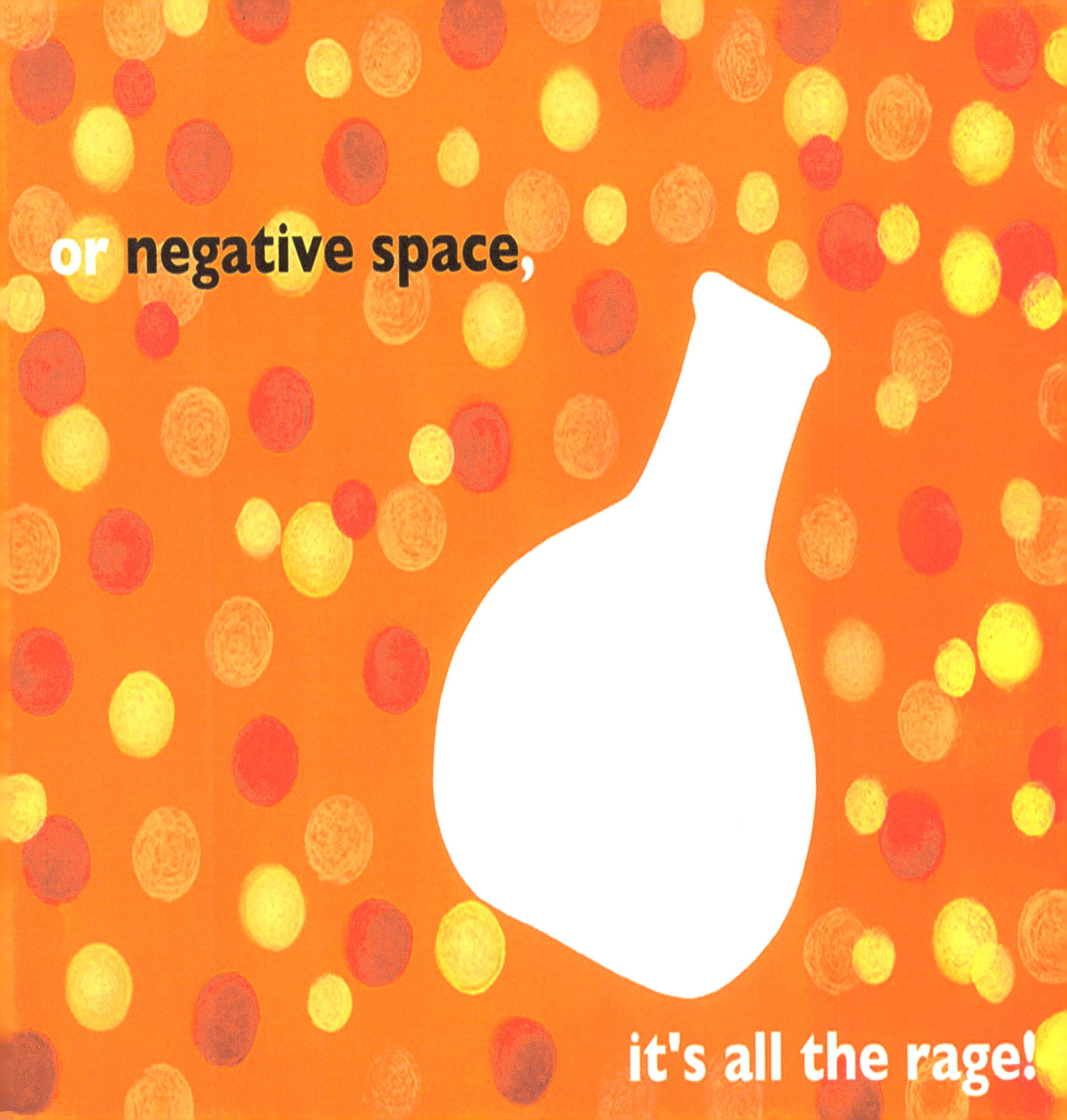
or negative space,
it's all the rage!

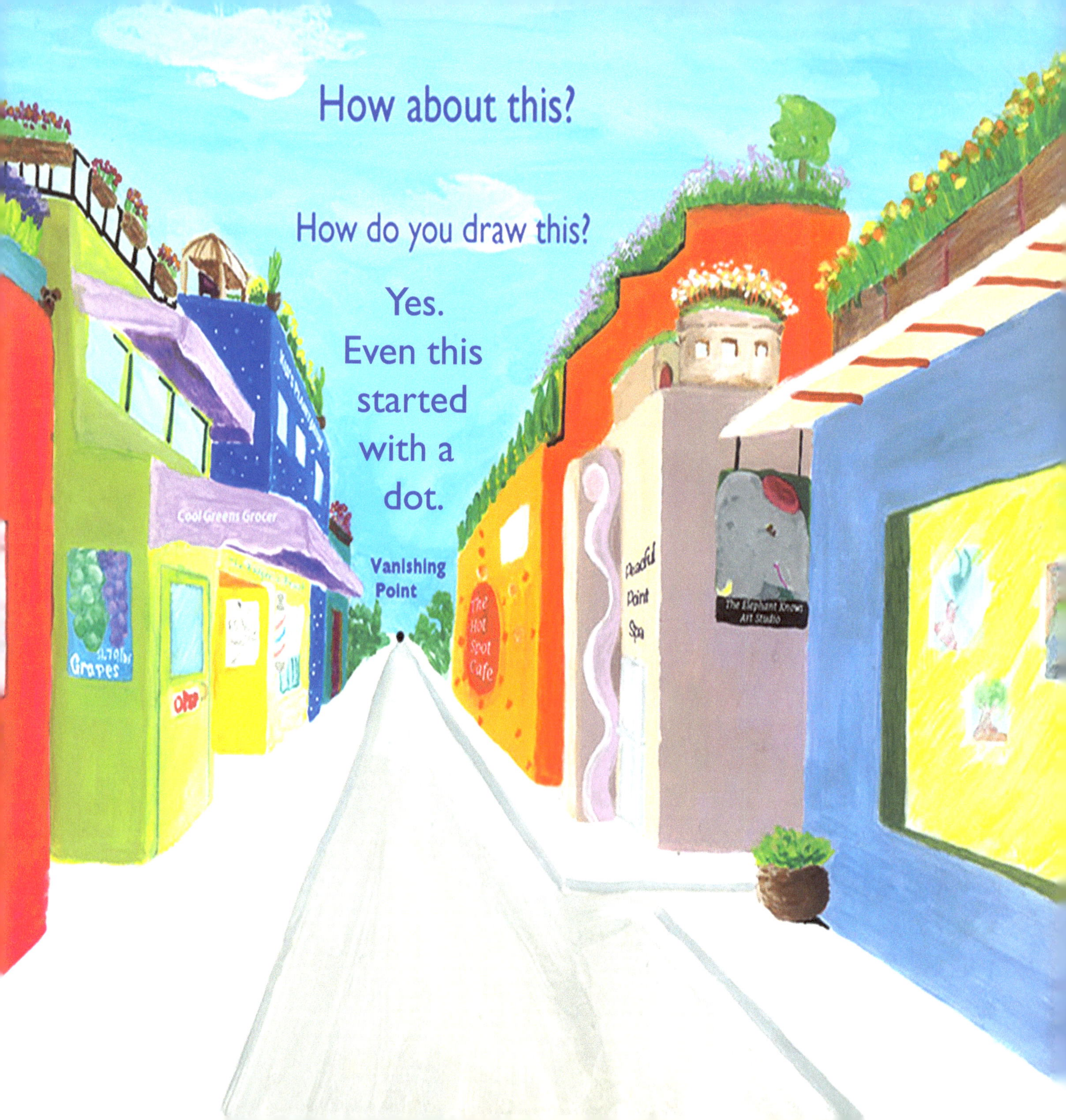


How about this?

How do you draw this?

Yes.
Even this
started
with a
dot.

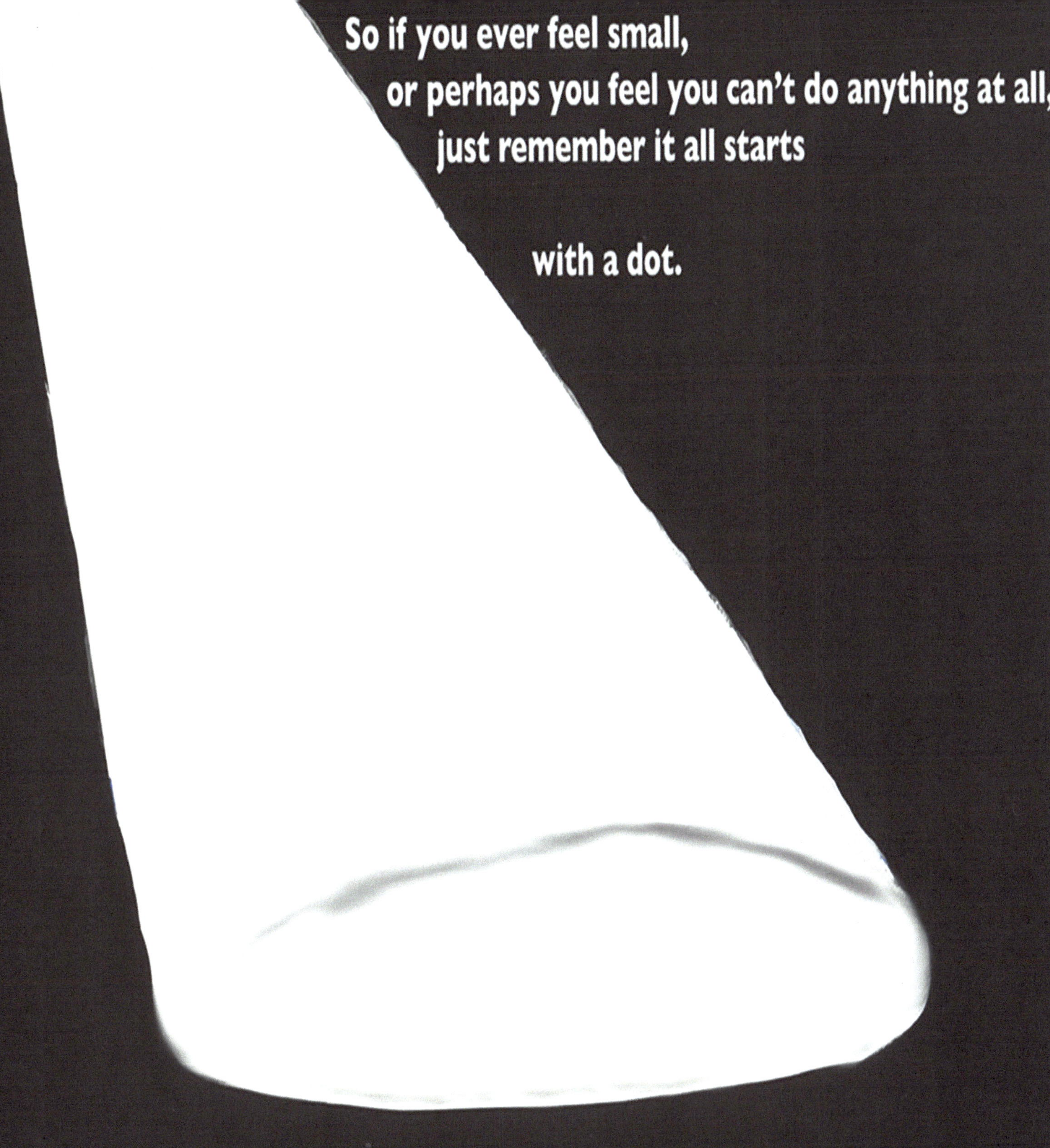
So if you ever feel small,
or perhaps you feel you can't do anything at all,
just remember it all starts
with a dot.

# Glossary

| | |
|---|---|
| 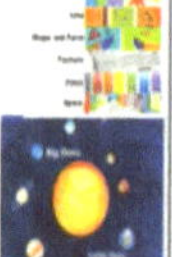 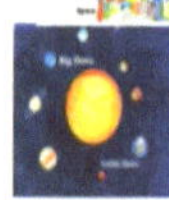 | **The elements of art** are the basic building blocks of a piece of art. They are color, line, shape, form, texture, value, and space.<br>**The solar system** consists of the sun and all the planets and gravitational objects that orbit the sun. The most well known planets are Mercury, Venus, Earth, Mars, Jupiter, Saturn, Uranus, Neptune, and dwarf planet-Pluto. Hint to remembering these planets: "**M**y **V**ery **E**xcellent **M**other **J**ust **S**erved **U**s **N**ine **P**izzas." |
| 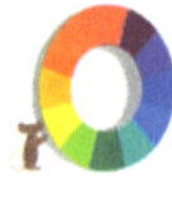  | **Color** is the element of art that is produced when light strikes an object and is reflected back to the human eye. A color has hue (color name), intensity (strength) and value (lightness or darkness of a color). Primary colors are red, blue, and yellow. Secondary colors are purple, orange, and green.<br>**Neutral Colors** are the combination of complementary color pairs, which produces gray. Black, white, gray, and brown are considered neutral colors. |
| 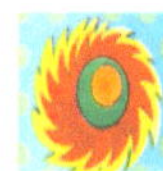 | **Complementary Colors** are any two colors that are opposite each other on the color wheel: 1. Red and green, 2. Orange and blue, 3. Yellow and purple. These pairing provide high contrast and are very vibrant combinations. |
| 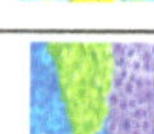 | **Cool Colors** are blue, green, and purple. They convey calmness in artwork. Cool colors tend to recede (move back). |
| 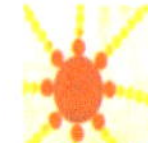 | **Warm Colors** are red, orange and yellow. They convey vibrancy in artwork. Warm colors tend to advance (jump out). |
| 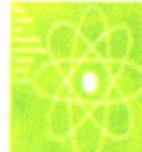 | **The Atom** is the basic building block of all matter. Matter is anything that takes up space. |
| 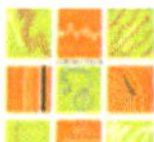 | **Line** is the path made by a moving point.<br>**Vertical line** is a line that goes straight up and down.<br>**Horizontal line** is a line that goes from left to right or vice versa.<br>**Diagonal line** is a slanted line other than perpendicular or horizontal.<br>**Perpendicular lines** are two lines that intersect/cross at a 90-degree angle.<br>**Line segment** is a part of a line that has two end points.<br>**Line ray** is a line that has one end point and goes off in one direction into infinity.<br>**Parallel lines** are two lines that are side by side and will never intersect/cross.<br>**Directional lines** are lines that are used to show direction.<br>**Expressive lines** convey feeling or energy. |

| | |
|---|---|
| | **Shape** is an enclosed area that has two dimensions- height and width. Shapes are flat. Shapes can be geometric. These are shapes are mostly made up of straight lines, like squares, triangles, rectangles, pentagons, hexagon, heptagon, octagon, etc. Shapes can be organic. These shapes may be irregular and are generally found in nature like animals or trees. |
| | **Form** is an enclosed space that has three dimensions - height, width and depth. Forms can stand on their own. Examples of forms are cube, sphere, cylinder, and rectangular prism. |
| | **Texture** is the way the surface of something feels when touched. Texture can be actual or visual. Actual texture refers to the fact that an object has a real texture that can be touched. Visual texture is the implied texture created by the illusion of a painting or a drawing. |
| | **Value** is the lightness or darkness of a color created by adding either white or black to that color. Tints are the light values of a color. Shades are the dark values of a color. |
| | **Space** is the distance around, between, below, and within an object. This is usually characterized by two-dimensional, (2D), or flat space. However, in art, the illusion of three-dimensional space, (3D), can be created with various techniques like aerial perspective, one-point perspective, two-point perspective, and three-point perspective.<br>**Positive Space** is the area the subject of the artwork occupies. In a picture of a bookshelf, the bookshelf is the positive space.<br>**Negative space** is the space around and between an object. For example, the space around a bookshelf and between the shelves is the negative space. |
| | **Aerial perspective** is a general approach to creating the sense of depth in a drawing. Simply put, things that are drawn large, low on the page, in brighter color, with greater detail look closer to the viewer. Overlapping objects is also a general principle of this approach. So size, placement on the page, color, and details affect the illusion of space created on a flat piece of paper. |
| | **One-Point perspective** is a mathematical system to create the illusion of space. The major lines of a drawing meet at the vanishing point. The vanishing point is the farthest point in the drawing and everything else is drawn in relation to this point. |

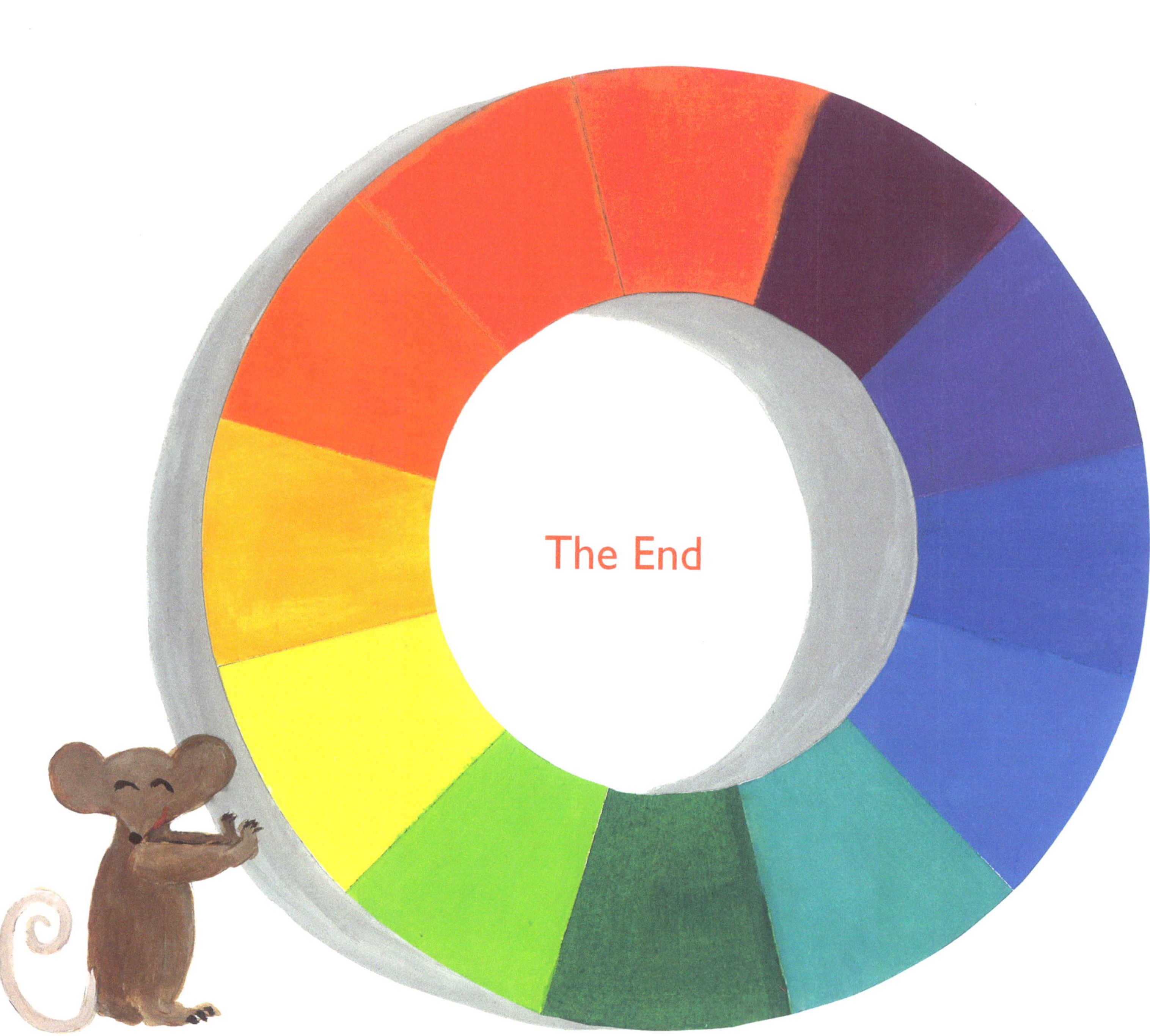
The End

www.ingramcontent.com/pod-product-compliance
Lightning Source LLC
LaVergne TN
LVHW070205110826
845147LV00002B/504

*9780988603011*